CIRCLING THE SQUARE

Michael Hamburger

Circling the Square

POEMS 2004–2006

ANVIL PRESS POETRY

Published in 2007
by Anvil Press Poetry Ltd
Neptune House 70 Royal Hill London SE10 8RF
www.anvilpresspoetry.com

This book is published with financial assistance
from Arts Council England

Designed and set in Monotype Ehrhardt by Anvil
Printed and bound in England
by Cromwell Press, Trowbridge, Wiltshire

ISBN 978 0 85646 392 1

A catalogue record for this book
is available from the British Library

CONTENTS

2006

ACKNOWLEDGEMENTS AND A NOTE

Some of these poems have appeared in the following periodicals:

Agenda, *The European English Messenger* (Finland), *Irish Pages* (Belfast), *Konzepte* (Germany), *The Liberal*, *The London Magazine*, *Neue Zürcher Zeitung* (Switzerland), *Poetry Salzburg Review* (Austria), *Stand*, and *Waxwing Poems from the House of Icarus* (Ireland).

Unable as I found myself to place the contents in any thematic order, let alone classify them by form or kind, this time I opted for a chronological sequence – in the mere hope that this knows better than I just how one poem connects or contrasts with another. (Titles are no clue to that either, if poems with the same title – like those called 'Aging', begun many years ago and contin-ued at various stages of the process – were not conceived as a coherent sequence or whole.) The one exception in this book is 'Air on a Shoe-String', written in 2006 and placed as a warning to my readers of what follows.

AIR ON A SHOE-STRING

Ah, Music, Poesie
To which one could aspire!
'Higher' things formerly
Now pronounced 'hire'.
Into my street-soiled hat
Hardly one coin is dropped,
Rarely a bite for the belly –
Because their ears are stopped
With so much talkie-telly –
Tele- that's lost its vision,
Doles out celebrity
Mixed up beyond derision,
Become advertisement
For this and this and that
All grown indifferent,
Mashed into salesman-chat.

Laugh if this instrument
For other use was meant:
Jews' harp it once could be,
Not boosted, amplified
For puffed inanity,
But silence, like din, defied.

Bad penny perhaps at best,
I circulate, can't rest:
Against the pitter-patter
In traffic, icy rain,
Twanging, turn up again
Only to prove: no matter,
As long as the making's true –
Of tunes or of a shoe –
To do what I must and can.

2004

LATE JANUARY MORNING

From east and north deduce
The still dubious light
Until, risen above the roof,
It glints on the southern horizon,
Tints bare tree-trunks, budding,
Rims with haloes the blackness
Conifers hug to their cores.

Against this coldest wall,
High window's misted panes
Last summer's last-lingering rose
With petals half-unpacked
Waves to a cryptic season,
None we can call our own
Whom each old friend's death leaves darkened,
Dimness of younger eyes
Grown too listless for seeing.

The blizzard-borne snow
Forecast for the week, will it shine?
More prescient, soil has allowed
Primrose to flower, aconite, snowdrop,
From burial will resurrect them
Bodily, though they droop.

And inch by inch, this morning,
Watched, the rimed lawn turns green.

A NIGHTMARE

... From nowhere he makes for me,
This blank-faced anybody,
Hands me a fat floppy book.
Paperback? So it seems
Till the front cover splits
Horizontally when I turn it
In search of a contents list,
Reminder of what those might be.

'Your poems at last,' he proclaims.

Flicking through, I see
My rejected drafts of decades
Forgotten long ago,
Ragbag so thoroughly stuffed
That even the pagination
Is that of discarded sheets
And I can't tell how many
Or which the scavenger found.

'What?', I burst out, just able
Not to hurl the bundle at him,
'You've published my waste paper basket,
No, a dustbin more capacious
Left unemptied outside a house
Disowned, untenanted;
Didn't warn, consult me,
Sent me no contract, no proof.

So much for the author-ship,
This pirate vessel, leaky.

Before one passenger
Pays for your ego-trip
Do me another favour:
An unremovable strip
Over the punished name:
For ever make it stick.'

He cringes, says nothing more.
In silence rage subsides
Into questioning, pity:

'Or don't – on second thoughts –
But shame the vanity
Of loving that made to last.
These might-have-beens, too, were mine,
My refuse, my abortions;
And what in the long run lasts longest
Is oblivion, nameless or named.
So thank you. Forgive the blame.'

TERMINAL TOUR

I

'Stay put', she said. 'This is it.
Starting–point, destination
Both Nowhere on your tickets.
Sit in the lounge – or quit
If a car for your recall
Was parked by you or summoned.
Your luggage? It's too light
For our scale's registration.
How, why, by whom this flight
Was booked, computerized
We have no means to tell.'

'Nor I. So thanks. Amen
To every complication.
Just let me share again
Air hostess litanies
Of safety, of salvation,
Jet organ introit,
A choir's unearthly swell,
The stop marked vox humana
Become angelical;
And clouds reversed in ice-light
Perversely let me praise.'

2

Landed indeed, I blink at the white and gold
Of so much baroque, such plump angels tumbling,
Walk what I'm told is the Prater, where nearly sixty years
    back
On leave from alpine service, more wondering
I strayed from the Hotel Sacher, conquerors' rest-house
    then,
Street map redundant now, guidebook discarded –
Indirection will see me through, between no–more and
    not-yet –
Among the few faces recognized, the many half-placeably
    strange
And these at work here once, removed, if not for ever.

Then off cross-country through plains past hills to high
    summits,
Through towns with names just remembered and names
    never noted,
Flashes of rail-side wildflowers, their guessed-at shapes
Blacked out too soon by tunnels –
Though the train also sang, hosannas,
Polyphony wordless from bass to descant,
Diapason for blocked ears, fulfilled in its fading.

3

But herded again, penned in
For departure; a little hitch
In transit, the first 'plane detained,
A zigzagging sprint through the maze of gates,
The right leg, aching, intent
On late retirement, the left,
Its grim propeller, bereft
And, oh, the one bag heavier –
But the craft already boarded,
Four hours to kill till the next,
A driver waiting in vain and leaving
On the other side of the sea
For the thirty-mile final stretch.

Nowhere once more. Blankness,
Dusk, advertisement-lit
While on the unseen, foreknown
Inaccessible city outside
Not wholly homogenized yet
The real sun shines.

DOMESTIC

I

'Hardly a fantast, except in dreams,
All sorts of things you put into your poems,
Their auras, their mutations, vanishings –
But out of doors – by preference, evasion?
Now verse, while you can, the habitation too
Called yours for some three decades,
Not a herbarium, this time, nor a zoo.
For once pick an interior. Let us in.'

Into a medley of anachronisms?
Being not one but many succesive mixtures
Of styles, materials, fixtures,
Hotchpotch, some of it botched, of odds and ends,
Amalgam of five centuries or so
Dream-gathered for his father-in-law-to-be
By an eccentric poet-painter-architect
Adding a studio wing
To labourers' cottages durably plain?
And the full inventory that would bore
Anyone save an agent, auctioneer
Or TV archaeologist breathless in glib surprise
That there's a past, flashed into and out of eyes,
Into and out of ears already surfeited?

Reduction, blanks, restriction
Make readable both history and fiction:
Fragments are what we know –
Even of our own selves: they come and go.
Habits of beauty, skill and expectation?
Sudden and slow is perception's way.

Wandering sunbeam at play
On leaves indifferent yesterday,
This crest, these branches fed
By roots in darkness, never dug up till dead.

2

Well it's a listed building. Listed for what,
Often we've wondered. Could it be
That inconveniences so multifarious,
So cumulative make it a rarity?
Tudor garage, unheatable, and adjoining
Tudor bread oven, bricked over, defunct
In deference to an AGA cooker
Converted to oil, if later, for labour-saving,
Hot water piped to the lion-legged bathtub upstairs.

That garage, though, on a bend in the lane
Asks for collision by speed or stealth –
Experienced once, since when it serves
As an apple-store from autumn to spring...

If, curious, you search the middle cottage,
In a sitting-room closet you'll find
Proof that the Jacobeans, too, baked bread,
With that enrichment can load your head:
A second bread oven flue, dear to our cats;
Also, that leaded panes were made to last,
Like the wide hardwood floorboards,
Oak beams perennially wood-wormed, yet firm –
Unlike their deal replacements, brittle with rot...

An expert recently revealed
Signs of a late mediaeval pre-existence –

Intuited perhaps by the conflating architect
When in the 1920 studio he installed
A stone baronial mantelpiece of that period –
Genuine or replica the smoke-stains have concealed.

As for the after-life,
It's marked by a water-pump inscribed 1770 –
A date not indifferent to me, never mind why...
Or the various underground cisterns,
Why, when and where they were lined with care,
What need or luxury they supplied –
Rain water pumped into his lady's bath
By the late Colonel, our predecessor
Who to a gossipy Rector calling
Would say: 'I'll give you five minutes, Padre'...

3

Oh, this eccentric house –
A bit of everything, with gadgets that were modern
In 1920 or in 1930,
Now worn, senescent, dirty.
That studio was partitioned, central heating conducted
To part of the whole, still never warm in winter,
Source of the latest loss:
A leaking radiator, senile, that in our absence
Drenched the box files of irreplaceable papers
Left on the floor of the library it became.

So fondness has turned ironic,
Rhymes it comes up with limpingly Byronic
While we bear with them still, the drudgery, damage,
        bother,
Indulge them as one does a great-grandmother

In her third childhood… bustle on, though lame…
And could bleat on till silenced – but for shame.

4

Beyond the studio annexe, where the lane is straight
Stands that on which I'll concentrate:
A Nissen hut, crass utility plonked there
For a real war, the house requisitioned
As a rest-home for men commissioned
And more or less disabled –
Their attendants also to be housed or stabled –
Then, when the Colonel had bought the place,
He a handyman, contraption-maker,
A rusting memorial, transmogrified:
To him as good as listed,
Spacious enough, besides, for lumber and recollection…
Yes, and a car – or two, were a second required.

Inside, on what were shelves or dumped the length of the
        walls,
More relics, of detritus, disuse,
Timbers, slats half-decayed,
Weatherboards, doors, broken mowers,
Tools that might have been mended,
Bamboo canes from the marsh, stacked there so long
That they themselves would need propping,
Glass covers for the coldframe whose brick foundations
Long ago crumbled away…

Sixty years on, it's nature again, naturalizing,
That hides, redeems the intruding eye-sore,
Holds together – how? – the convenient structure,
Corrugated iron curved double sheets of the roof

Patched with plastic surrogates, rust-free, that crack,
Camouflaged now for a truce of sorts, sealed
By a cover of evergreen ivy,
Clouded in June with the clustered white
Of the most potent of rambler roses, tiniest multiflora.

True, no more swallows bravely whizzing
To their nests through a gap in the panes,
No more stove recalled from other rank service
That made such barrack room huts a home,
Floor palliasse our bedding –
Unless on groundsheets we slept out of doors,
Only canvas for shelter
And – neither stove nor dry ration carried –
With a bayonet filched a turnip,
Raw grub, from some farmer's field…

A hint, for you, of continuity
Which furniture, too, attests, and an archive salvaged
From wreck, disruption, deep forgetfulness –
But every salvaged thing threatened again by the sea…

5

Do I let you in?
So far, no farther, friend,
Halting, halted before the end of a story
That can no more end than begin…

Histories, mysteries, whether our own or another's
We took over, lived in, conserved where we could
And, if we can, shall pass on,
These tenants, too, gone.

The rest, much more, I must withhold,
If by interior you meant confession:
Vain words are poison worse than indiscretion,
From which a truth can spring, to one grown old,
The too much of a life untellable – if not already told
By intimation of what's intimate,
Mere moments, always, that could centre
Slow years, slow centuries of this eccentric house
Whose dubious core not you nor I can enter.

6

How did it come about, this tenancy?
Need you ask? – Absurdly, foolishly:
Random fancy first, then obdurate grimness,
Defiant, or loyalty as perverse
As blessing, sustenance capsuled in a curse.

It was a mulberry tree,
Centenarian at least, that seduced us buyers,
Made us the occupiers
Of what went with it, nobody sane would touch,
As the surveyor warned, dissuading us,
Listing the defects for clients deaf to such:
So mixed, these modesties are ruinous,
This minimality will prove too much...

An infamous hurricane laid our landmark flat,
Half the root ripped, the bulk and leafage sprawling
On flowerbed, lawn and path – a surgical case,
One upright branch only spared from sawing, lopping
In hope that the half-root, trunk's torso now prostrate
Might still sustain just that.

They did, made more of less,
New growth, new fruitfulness,
Out of near-death by amputation
Let a poor nucleus live.

And there's one positive
For you, within a wry narration,
Inaudible pulse within the real estate,
Unlisted throb, unlistable, unhoused.

TOWARDS EQUANIMITY

Brightest July between the darkenings
But cold, as though a waiting now for autumn,
Winter again, perhaps another spring
Of jonquils drenched, plum blossom perishing,
Ripped by the winds at war.

If light behind the eyes
Refuses eager reciprocity,
Dimmer it was before,
Blacked out against the bombers,
So spared the recognition
By searchlight of their mission
To set ablaze or, blasting, raze the house.

Seeing, from first to last,
Is a response to the sun,
Sun's moon at least, far glitter
From some more alien planet.
No war was total, no window wholly blind
While one night's candle guttered.

The stored light, memory's,
Can that sustain a seeing?
A film's, it flashes by
Faster than breath, than any creature's being,
Human or butterfly.

Here, our survival's house,
Rot grows preposterous.
Outside, wronged nature breeds
Thicker and denser weeds,
In limbs a weariness, cross-fire of pain
Leave late exertions vain –

To antiquated lovers, you and me
Through clash and crash and clutter
Still, too, the morning sky
Earthlight of evening primrose opening,
At night cow's moan, owl's cry,
Homed? heard? remembered? hints of house martins'
    mutter.

Timor mortis? Too well
I have rehearsed the going,
Before the bombs fell learned
That loss of love not life was their undoing
Who young were numbed, conscripted to the hell
That turns to dusk each dawn –

Yet need not, did not when
Half-blinded we faced fire,
By rote, by regimen,
Behind blank eyes for fire's sake, for the sun's,
Though that fire could go out, all light withdrawn.

Recurrence even calls
For change behind the eyes;
From births and burials
A blur of strangeness clings
To long familiar places, features, things.
Dredged up with flux deposits, they surprise.
Re-hung, this drawing of you girlish gathers
Meaning from all you've been.

Lingering now, we're blessed
With slowness, let eyes rest
On continuities,
Darknesses, lights that mingle and seem one,
So many we have seen.

HER BIRTHDAY'S WEATHER

Mulberry stain, purple, on fingers fumbling
For a September dessert of earth, wood savours
Grittily sweet – to feet stumbling
Over roots exposed in a hurricane
Drops of blood-dark juice, no matter now
Whether a tree's, a man's or woman's,
The first and last of long marriage
All mixed in this day's light,

Azure so pure, refracted
By dragonfly wings at rest
Glittering, late, as though denying
Departure of more than leaves, ever,
Where limbs, trunks too have been dying.

If still gathering, garnering, sowing –
To serve whose meal, what need? –
With one word, fumbling, we could reach the hub
Of such conjunction, then
It would be our unknowing
That melted it, put the picked name to shame.

AGING V

(For J.S.)

Our minute-hands, warped, slow down,
The days accelerate,
Long distance runners who lapped or lapping
Strain for the finishing line
That marks them out for stillness.

So round the seasons, above,
Clouds race or, drifting, shift,
Break for the exceptional sun.
Rarely seen or heard since May,
By late September, now
The high-flying swifts must be gone,
But a rhododendron flowers.

Time? The currency
Microchips mint, apportion
As they do status, fame.
Whatever we do, leave undone,
Our weeks have shrunk to days:
Spectators at our own game,
We can't care enough to count,
On the lean runner, the strapping
Dreamily, cloudily gaze.

Nonagenarian friend,
My first of the scribblers' tribe,
Brave runner forgotten in London,
Shuffling on there, do you
Watch clouds in your blocked-out sky,
Warmed when the sun breaks through?
Or what, while dead words dance
Remains your sustenance?

AGAINST BRIGHTNESS

Towards winter, my hearing blocked,
Air empty of song-thrush, blackbird,
What is it that cries out
From my bow-saw, moans, then screams?
The blade's toothed metal, mindless,
Dead wood of an ash-tree's limb shed?
Their friction, of course, mechanical
As bullets fired into a body
Quite still but may-be not killed enough
Where it's weapons that have their will –
Loud now, strident, as if
Earth matter had found a voice
To pound through the sieve of ears never open
Its pith, violation's pain.

Worse, when the work is done
Silence will mend again,
Our lowland mountain range, cloud,
Dissolving, make way for sunrays
Which halo the higher leaves not yet fallen.
Later, the logs, aglow,
With innocent warmth will soothe us,
Their mite of residue
So light, so nearly white,
It can merge in each day's dust.

BRITISH SUMMER TIME SUSPENDED

1

This morning of the day before
We wake to weird penumbra, more
The westering moon's, full-bodied, clear
Than the blurred sun's – as though the very season,
Grown weary, mingled dawn with night,
The generator bleary, not our sight,
A matted silver-greyish-white
Colour enough for things of earth and air,
Contour enough for tree-crests leaved or bare.

2

Well, even to pure reason,
To Einstein as to Plato,
Time was a hot potato.
Not so to impure reason, politics
Long wise to nature and her mocking tricks:
Uncertainty is what few minds can bear.
So cut the knot with clocks,
Suppress the paradox.
Just wind back by one hour
Those minute-hands, ignoring that their power,
If microchip-driven, too may lack
Resistance to a two-way track.
The winders then will rise
To serviceable roads and skies
Through which to travel with no need to know
What makes the wheels turn, why they come and go.
In function is their peace,

Their profit, their increase
And by conjunction function is imposed.
So Bob's your uncle and the matter closed.
By dot-com, radio, tabloid, box,
In every type and clef,
To babies, morons, lunatics and crocks,
Alzheimer cases, yes, the blind and deaf
The change must be conveyed:
'All that was given now is made.
Yet as a hand-out we confer
This benefit on him and her,
This abstract panaceic sticking-plaster,
Tiktox, your synchronizing comforter
That will kiss better pains, allay disaster
Throughout the next half-year.'

3

Gobbledygook reigns over nothingness,
Murkier mornings, day's duration less,
No energy saved while in the earlier dark
Lamps glare on workers, flood their crammed car park.

As for disaster, it's such chronic fare
That without condiments we've ceased to taste or care.
Judgement closed down, 'For Sale' on the gates of Hell,
Science feeds headlines with a parallel,
Global and hyper-global crash
Boosts news consumption, rakes in still more cash,
Eccentric orbit, meteor, eclipse
Whet a cloyed hunger for apocalypse.

4

In natural halflight, though, I strum
This desultory ricercar
Through 'were' and 'will-be', 'can-be' back to basic 'are',
Old age that leaves a life's curriculum
As labyrinthine, entrance, exit, end
Dubious, subverts all fixed chronology.

Where am I when I pause from verse to tend,
Still, our wild garden of remembered flowers,
The sown, self-seeded, dormant, posthumous,
The once or not yet 'ours',
Their names dissolved, their provenance forgotten?
In jumble humbled there, I'm free,
While labouring, to let them be
Playthings of mutable light that's lent to them and me;

Return then to this bay, in drift my anchorage,
For words a landing-stage,
The roof about to crack, window-panes rotten –
A place reliable as the winds, the sea
From which, in its old age, it harbours me,
So that with loose anachronistic rhyme
I may defy fictitious time,
Found in the maze a round economy
Of loops, of indirection overcome,
Chime on through summer time suspended
With nothing, nothing ended.

EAST SUFFOLK LIGHTS, LATE NOVEMBER

Maple leaf-coloured from fallen foliage
Cock pheasants come out to forage
Among medlars frost-ripened, dropped from the tree.
From long occlusion sunbeams emerge
On to rime that reflects them,
Make a wake for the deepened red
Of one lingering blossom, sparaxis
Limp at last, lying flat.

But high on the house
A climber decades old
Against moon coldness opens rose-coloured petals –
Pale when the evening skies
With amber, cornelian, vermilion to scarlet
Rim clouds drifting eastward
From the western, southern on fire.
Lower, through hedgerows darkening
An aquamarine never summer's glows.

MAGPIE PALINODE

Marauders, infanticides
Too humanly once I traduced them,
Fell into symbol, seduced,
Reduced to black and white
Hints of a steel-blue sheen,
Glints too of other tints
In their eyes, their casing plumage,
Saw no grace in their hopping, grounded

As this resident pair, come down
On to the garden table
For dole, strewn winter seed:
They defer to a pheasant's hunger,
Curbing their own, their cunning,
Let little finches flit
At pickings that fit their need,
Collared doves, more cautious feeders
Wait for a share unthreatened

This day, the year's darkest, shortest,
Ambers withheld above, hesitant azure
Translucent in cumulus calm
And the rimed grass responding:
Their chatter muted, they halt
All glib judicial weighing,
Beyond the here, the now for paragon
From far off seemingly
Fetch home that Ugandan egg
Which, trodden on, cracked, absolves
Killers in any cause,
Releases them into peace.

2005

ONE OR MORE

Full moon on Christmas Night,
All were aware who walked here
From, to parked cars, arriving, leaving,
Our children long grown separate but near,
Their children, searchers, now least knowable
When gathered in one house,
The eldest due soon to take off
For countries far as can be to stretch her compassion.

Four times I looked, four times I saw
Four moons – one brightest, round,
About it, firmly haloed, aureoled,
Outlined, three segments not concentric.
Superimposed, they seemed, so separate
That into other space they might have drifted,
Each spectral, each bright enough,
If by reflection only,
To make another moon, believable,
The dark of this night so clear
No cloud of witness could diffuse their shining.

With and without my glasses recently renewed
I looked, said what I saw.
They may have smiled and thought:
Have your eyes tested again – and then your brain.
Is it you or your moons that are eccentric?
Said nothing there, though still the youngest
Could laugh when the old crackpot spoke.
She sensed this was no joke

Of his who, to make sure, next morning gazed
At a moon dimmed by daylight,

Apocryphal moon outshone
By the invisible sun:
Still four, not one, the fainter circles glinted.

So once the sun had split
Not here, in icelight, colder,
For intruders lured by the bluest white
To see what none had seen,
Some dazzled into their dying:
When common senses failed
More turned against them,
They brought equipment, impetus of dogs,
Common sense, too, the basic science shared.
Last rations had run out,
Stalled what had launched and driven them, the consensus
That seeing is believing.

Christmas moon waned here, fading,
Children grandchildren removed
Into their choices, their imaginings,
Their explorations, polar, equatorial
Or temperate urban merely,
But plural now wherever
In earth-perplexity
Nearer and nearer, deadlier,
I leave cosmology
To those who mumble, those who shout
As palliative a creed or doubt,
From vision first, then formula construe
Fallible empires of the for-ever true.

Soon my seen moons may roll
Back to their matrix, four into one,
Or from an Essene scroll,
Belatedly found, a luminous link accrue.

While I have eyes they'll be
Map-makers of a mystery –
The little they can see
Thanks mainly to the sun.

If, distant reader, you
The nearest, farthest take
And leave it, make
Of these moons what you please
Or what you can, in your uncertainties,
In your unknowingness, my work is done.

AGING VI

The wonder of it: to rise again,
Daily still at the day's first light
For love of this winter air
Filled with the more grown less,
A copious emptiness,
Anyone's, no one's now;
Rise from the dregs fetched up
Nightly of fermentations
Long ago drained:
Impendings, implosions, ecstasies,
Promiscuous lumber hoarded,
Perpetuum mobile
Past faces of the dead, in dream alive,
Through nameless places, never to arrive
Until awake, defying
The weight of all those years,
Gravity's pull to the grave,
To drink, bath, dress –
And labour on, while aching limbs obey,
Maintain the overreaching tree,
Dig, plant, sow, lop, saw, clear.
Whether or not they visit, both inaudible,
Goldcrest's thin solo, peewit's one call outsings
Polyphonies of centuries in the head;
So for whatever ear
Keep a frail silence fed.

THE WAY AND ITS POWER

(i.m. Arthur Waley)

Reading the Tao Te Ching
In February spring
I see a crocus ring
Raised by this fickle light
With petals folded, never opening.
Could heaven's moods, the weather
Mock their obedience, smile
Politically at them, to beguile?
That order, too, be power
Inflicted on a flower
Flimsy as daymoth or a dove's breast-feather?

Still earlier aconite
Fulfilled itself despite
True winter's colder light,
Hellebore too, the purple and the white,
Primrose precociously,
Quite out of season one mauve honesty.

Yet, nearly nameless, he and his way were right
For all such botany.
If by his negative
The non-assertion of identity
Trans-human we could live
Most positive that would be.
Feeding wild birds we tend their tiniest feather
But without force leave petals to their plight.

The paradox sets us free:
Making our way through power's uncertainty,

Homing to dark no sunbeam will unfold,
Humbled at last could hold
The more than his ten thousand things together.

LIMITS

Ten days or more of snow, frost, hail
On to crocuses furled for a spring suspended,
North winds to pull them down.
A thaw's intermission, mere drizzle come,
Still they were white or mauve,
Almost they rose again, waiting for light.

Six yearling pheasants, foraging,
Lone squirrels, best-equipped
Of snatchers, diggers in any weather –
And the walnut trunk so near! –
For once have let them be.

As for humanity,
Gautama even postponed his nirvana
Till he could pass it on,
Thunder applaud his last words
Wafted to breed in the silence he'd fathered –

In which one laugh was heard:
Black Mara's, assured
That beneath the most radiant of yellows
His own darkness lurks, immortal;
That the Lion's teeth lifted by winds
Were dandelion seed
And the wisest of buddhas, all pain's eliminator
Had likened himself to a wheelbarrow patched,
Bits of string and wire binding the bodywork,
Yes, and defiance pushing it to its end
As long as the wheel creaked on.

Deeper snow has covered the crocus bed
And hardened overnight.
If invisibly now or never
A calyx releases its core's red-gold
To the limits it will have resisted.

AGING VII

On long vacation, year in, year out,
Residual guests in a once grand hotel,
We busy ourselves, planning the day's distractions
From vacuous repetition, seasonless:
Something a little different on our plates,
Exchange of words more and more strenuous,
For happening, real event
A voice from the past not silenced yet, gasping.

Or, wilder waters too far behind,
Goldfishes in a garden pond
That's plastic-lined
We linger on, contentedly confined,
Bred in a tank, need yearn for no beyond
But lurk, dart, wriggle while we can
Within a leaking inwardness, our dwindling span.

Else, conservationists
Of some patch small or larger we call home,
Servants of earth to the last,
With failing finger-joints, arthritic,
Legs that had lugged equipment for miles on forced
    marches,
Then released, for a lark slogged from London to Cornwall,
Worn out at the hip now, kneel as in prayer
To let through light for seedling, sapling planted,
Less than half-remembered, found under weeds by
    searching
That it may live, outlive our care –
Although it cannot, merged in the natural flux,
Razed by the murderous, bulldozing money's.

Further loss, worse, withheld, all must be well:
Defiance like acceptance leaves it so.
With given tongues only could we curse
Or, humbled, hold them, wiser.

Enough that in late June,
After such clotting cloud, ice winds that shrivelled
Apple leaves newly shaped
Our sky has cleared again – and is not ours.

COMBAT. CONTEST. MATCH

On battlefield, arena, hard court, grass,
The screened green baize, it must be single:
Promoted with multiple noughts to a million
May qualify for myth, its potency.

Odds must be even, the protagonists matched
As Hector with Achilles
And, when they meet, Helen not here nor there,
The *casus belli* swallowed up in the act,
Land, gold, oil barrels, money,
Conglomerate power, celebrity – all brittle –
Subsumed in the pure clash of hero-monsters.

If, woman or man, out of quick senses one
Propels whatever weapon,
The other by deliberate procrastination
Twists mind and muscle separate until
Spontaneous sharpness blunts, speed's current fails,
The graced one fumbles, misses –
Though both may rise again from that ordeal
What weeps is the winner's shame.

THE WILD GARDEN RELEASED

To sift a season from this March-April-May,
From early June a turning,
Harsh winds, occluded skies forbade:
What breathed here was the melting poles,
What could not stir was bees.
Fruit blossom hung aborted,
Young apple leaves, bay leaves withered
While, weather-proof, immune,
Thistle, nettle, bramble, common cleaver,
Sedge and couch-grass edged their way on.
Where a path had been cut, then trodden along the water
    ditch
In the marsh once annually scythed
Indigenous orchids dormant for twenty years
Or invisible there
Haunted oblivion with pink and purple,
Never again the exotic cyclamen
Which for thirty years under a yew tree's blackness
From one corm had raised more than a hundred flowers –
Till ground elder roots crept closer...

Memory's lumber – those names, those names
Not even theirs but ours,
Millennial, global history of roses only
From brier and the multiflora white
That climbs, rips, grapples more ruthlessly
Than any weed, more grossly sends out suckers,
With fragrance too fills more of the air
Than massed wild meadowsweet –
To infinite artefacts, the latest of mutations
Or the surviving classics pampered by those who know
    them...

Up to the highest trees grown past our tending,
Trunk of the great crack willow we did not plant,
Skeleton monument of a century's bulk,
Older, the mulberry tree
Uprooted by hurricane and resurrected,
Beech, maple, oak, pine, cedar still alive,
The rarer that could outlive us if not felled –
Small arboretum, one love's extravagance,
Without it, mortuary of promiscuous timber, sprawling:
All had, all have their being.

Now that the most familiar names desert,
For your sake call that peace,
Let them go home to hide in manyness.
Though tall trees tremble, gasp,
Flickering flowers flash by,
Released, the garden unlearns
Half of its history,
The fall into human time,
Number, measure, name,
All but the mystery:
No clash of growth with decay,
No conquest or love-clasp
Clocked by mortality.

A black tom-cat turns to me
Still deeps, unsoundable eyes.
Skimming them, swimming, I'm back
In a long-lost childhood place
Where first I met that gaze
Beyond identity.
Yes, the cats have come and gone,
Their years our calendar –
The near face and the far
In their clear eyes are one.

YET AGAIN

In full morning's first hour, briefly
They line up on the wires,
End of August, our sky
A summer's at last
And the sallow's leaves falling.

When reliably here they had nested
In furnace room, shed one kind,
Under northward eaves the other,
Their small-talk, little twitter
Hardly listened for, assumed,
Swallows it was, swooping in
Through a gap in the window-panes
Less wide than their wing-span,
House martins muttering
That to us brought home the season.

Now from my bath I see them,
Left eye blacked out, vision so blurred,
The shapes, the colours flicker
Against the larger space
Dazzlingly bright, then dark, their flight will dare;
And they'll be gone before
Guesswork and memory, mixed,
Can fix them, ever, tell
The progeny of two nests not crumbled
Along the roof from that
Of neighbouring barn or byre.

Swifts, barely glimpsed
Twice this year, swirling
Over these parts, recalled

Their hundreds above Rome
Fifty-five years ago
Watched with my host long dead,
The Orkney-born who wherever he found himself,
A wonderer, found blessings.
Fierce aerial spirits
There they seemed, not even haunting
Colossal ruins below,
Palazzi, smooth office blocks
Indifferently alien to them,
Their resting, nesting places
Hidden always from us.

And now? 'He's a non-looker,'
My critic writes, 'lets the sounds
Make such sense as they can.'
May-be. But with working eyes met
Shadows, voids, in creatures, things
And their names. Never could meet
The source of unbearable light
Save broken on surfaces, features;
With working ears, a signalman's, heard
Hiatus, hesitation
In every surge and gamut,
Heard the flow begin, heard it subside.

So yet again these birds,
Cutters through currents the one,
The other more halting, buffeted,
Have congathered for their going.
And mixed I must leave them,
The never humanly grasped
But by netting, eating, not here.
No matter, then, if only,
Separate, both can return.

HOMO SAPIENS – HOMO FABER – HOMO RAPIENS

Here, now,
Late July,
Grey sky,
Wind north-easterly.
Not one butterfly
On buddleia umbels, rocking.
Soil dry,
Delicate leafage drooping:
But for dew-fall, drought.

From houses numbered,
Named, assessed,
Price-tagged like their tenants
Quite soon to be seasonless,
Through by-ways of translation,
Reproduction, print
To a patience far off,
Ancient China, its poets
I must resort –
Tourist, no more, denied
The slope of their brushstrokes,
The tremors, vibrancies.

Then almost it seems
That from a single hand
Issued the things of song
Across our calendar's turning –
Another date not for them to note.

Plum blossom, cherry blossom
For a still graspable spring,

Chrysanthemum, for autumn,
Mad mating dance of cranes,
Cries of cranes receding, up in the air –
Such tokens were enough,
Carved jade, cut bamboo,

Plain shapes for long use,
Intricate working of silk, of glazes
While dynasties, borders vanished,
Uncounted corpses littered
A land-mass no mind could map,
Floated down nobody's river.

Yes, they knew of them, each and all,
Scribes who had served the powers
Because they must, or powers themselves
By birthright; but, exiled by change or choice,
As anchorites channelled their loves,
Into drunkenness could unself,
Dissolve into snowlight, blankness.

Seasons of one condition,
Recurrence contained them,
Bedded their best and worst.

ELECTRONOCUTED

How Pascal would have shuddered
At this infinitude not of lights in space
Nor Babel tower aspiring to any heaven
But information fungus of our making
That over the global surface spreads so fast,
Ocean water no barrier,
That a global deal can be clinched
Before the board has assembled,
Mass destruction delivered
Before war is declared.
Web indeed, world-wide
Surrogate for the earth we were made for,
Super-Promethean gift to mankind,
Its uses, limitless,
Replacing those of hand, heart, head
Which lag behind, too slow for competition.

Pascal? Does he have a slot
Among the potential billions?
There's one with a forename like Blazes –
Long dead, long redundant,
Notable once because he could think!
Electronics do that for us,
Begin as a toy, still wondered at,
Explored with fumbling fingers,
Then whiz us from first to second childhood
So blandly, with so little effort
There'll be nobody here to shudder
At a screen gone blank for good.

DOWLAND AGAIN

Never I see her weep
At her bereavements or the plagues that creep
Across our Earth,
But playing, paying, praying she works to keep
A table laid for brief convivial mirth
Even in dearth.

It's I the labourer out of doors
Repeatedly returning
To those melodious tears he did not shed,
Drawn from a fountainhead
Not his at all, the cryptic metaphors,
Chromatic, for an aimless yearning:
What words are meant to mean
A chord melts down to one dark might-have-been.

These trees, shrubs, herbs that half a lifetime long
Here in our garden grew
Had proved so strong
They seemed perpetual, both old and new,
But now for lack of tending
Before the gardener his have reached their ending –
A death to be lived through,
Lacrimae rerum, rift beyond our mending
When everywhere
Rankly self-seeded kinds push out the rare.

Printed or not, scattered among the dead,
The piled-up papers, dormant his tones could lie
For centuries, unheard if seen or read,
Then, being no one's cry,

Nobody's dances now, rang out more poignantly.
So, by persistence in a small endeavour
Out of no more he made an ever –
And so does she
Smiling on absences bleak or black to me.

MARROWS, 2005

I

Three times I sowed them this year,
Three times planted out seedlings,
Dug in compost, from so-called late spring
To so-called early summer.
Overnight all but one of the first
Vanished, not a stump or shred
Left to mark their demise.
As for the second lot,
Genetically dwarfed,
They languished, barren, with male flowers only,
Not so much as courgette, zucchino
Borne on their dank bed.

September let through the sun.
And suddenly
The survivor, the reinforcements
Remembered their marrowness,
Mothered a baby or two not for rotting,
Even one that, hidden, matured
Under leaves that as greedily spread
As the first had been devoured;
And by October, cooling,
Ground frost already feared,
Their tendrils had climbed an apple-tree.

2

There, weeks later they cling. Ought I to wait
For a crop to corroborate
That plants know better than I
When to grow, when to die,
Whether to propagate
As advertised or late,
Provide or mock the grower
Shamed as a would-be knower?

In my blood-sap I sense
Their timing's competence,
In their autumnal rise
Can read more sun-lit skies –
My mad barometer
Of weather waves astir,
All maddened, all frenetic –
My floral clock, prophetic.

For labour that's reward
Fitter by far than swelled or stunted gourd:
Condoling here with air, earth, water blast
And loss, their season passed.
All but remembrance amid rubble stilled,
Extremity-bearers, now they are fulfilled.

LAST OR FIRST

Mauve-lucent at midday,
Deepest blue towards night,
Monkshood, a deadly bonus
In its dark corner for us
With those colours marks an end.
In another, primrose yellow,
The last or first, has opened,
One daisy, minute, on the lawn.

Islanded there we can sit
In sunbeams that, slanting, shift
Through bare branches, leafage retained
On beech, oak, maple still.
While it holds, this mild autumn light,
We drift, though motionless,
Our 'have been', 'shall be', 'are',
World's always, knowing's never
All mixed, all circular,
So with no need to stir,
Choose between glare and shade
Before a black cloud blots out the white
And in the wind we shiver.

THE WINTER VISIT

More sudden than any spring
Memory could invent, completion came
With November's full moon
In whose rays, their white hair gleaming,
Nonagenarian couple on sticks they hobbled
Off again from our door.

That morning for us who waited
Hoarfrost pallor it was,
The low sun through clouds aglow,
Death-coloured leafage retained –
Until towards noon a damped sky-blue,
Winter's radiance, took over,
A roof-top, a tree-top shone.

Dubious hours passed: inexplicably
They'd made a detour, stopped at the sea,
Parked on a sand-cliff marked for obliteration
As though for confirmation,
By looking, that sooner or later
This land, these walls would be water –
When he since youth had said:
'Best not to be born – or dead'
Yet worked, worked, worked, in his eighties jogged
To keep the current unclogged.

Then across sixty-five years
Of meetings, distances
Between blocked ears the talk
Hobbled, shuffled – his
Gasped out in whispers, for he
Was weary well before night

Of all flotsam about to sink;
Hers more enquiring, still bright
Against the now fading light:
Of completion, too, hard-won,
So little left to be done,
But the broken snagged journey taken,
The words unspeakable spoken
By presence alone, on this brink.

CIRCLING THE SQUARE

Onion, apple, yes,
Round fruit or oval
Of the round world,
Walnut's intricate lobes
Double-cased, curled
Foetally for its growth, undoing.

In the tall mirror, though, what?
Biped more bird than ape
Wingless, but armed, clawed.
Strutting upright, straight
Until curled up for sleep;
If Chinese Buddha-bellied
Must hide the bulge, ashamed.

More tree, then, dwarfed, that walks,
Wrenched from the rootstock, forked
Downward where it splits
Not quite half-way between
Ground matrix and crest,
Concave the navel only –
Straight lines for infinity,
Lines that will never meet.

For symmetry, cruel, the cross.
Rectangular frame, glass
Often enclosing, keeping untouched
The nothing rotund on it
Save the human head, drooping –
Haloed at best with a light borrowed
From sun, moon, stars, the spheres.

A dome's vaulted roof perhaps,
Pre-Gothic, above,
Windowless crypt below.

Beyond those, outside,
All's fidget, manipulation
Called 'news', called 'history'
By the inventors of time,
Fixers of criss-crossed ends,
Adders of noughts – round or oval! –
Billionfold to the diminution
Of this and that, the real and peculiar.

Onion, apple, egg.
Yes, they revolve, evolve
And perish patiently:
This blue-tit's curved underside,
Wavelet of yellow down
Here plopped into stillness,
This fallen trunk left to rot.

So slowly at last we can spiral,
There's no telling ascent from descent,
Perduration from change.

WINTER EVENINGS, EAST SUFFOLK

The sun's and our days are shortening
While before solstice the visible moon fills out,
What on these lowland wide horizons lingers
As though to reiterate, recall, is dusk:
On the south-western from flame to glimmer
Slowly the glow subsides
From scarlet to roseate, amber drifts and shifts
Or else to a strip of blue
Deeper than any a summer noon sustained.
If a black cloud hangs there it shines
Rimmed with departing light.

December's last leafage responds:
A red so dark on this maple
It's nightfall too, detained,
Wisps of pale yellow to ochre
On the rugosa stems wilting
As on those with buds for another year.

Then, moon not yet full, whole skies
Whether clouded or clear
Are silver tarnishing.

Never a night is total
Until our vision, dimmed,
Disowns the shapes, the shadows,
All colours mixed on palettes too far away.

2006

AGING VIII

Years in themselves count for little,
Even anachronism – like Doughty's, Hardy's:
The less they belonged to their eras
The truer they grew to their names.

When this Thomas, doubting celebrant
Of moorland, woodland passions wilder, darker
Than the agenda of drawing-room, board-room, office
Found his Tess too disturbing, his Jude too obscure
For lending library ladies, allotments in magazines –
Good riddance to those, to the laborious plotting,
Deadlines for massed mass-market words! –
Before Edward succeeded Victoria
He'd gone home, retired into verse.

Came the war that no one could win,
The progress of mechanized killing,
Came the blasting of every foundation.
Still he lived on, still would not budge,
Though that modernity made his quaintness quainter.

Time to be gone? Not till dismissed from service,
His winter ultimate in the ducts.

* * *

But what if memory
Moves lost among its landmarks,
Their meanings jumbled, signposts jerked awry,
Of the too many, in the wrong place houses
The early loved one, long ago buried?

All's present, all is past,
The new day's first light merges in the last.

Own up, old loiterer awake
At the train window of a lifetime dream
Through stations unrecognizably rebuilt,
The one closed down, the one demolished:
Your hugged realities,
Pressed into song, eked out for story-telling,
Picked up, made up, have become fiction.

Confusion trusted, though, can set you free
To laugh at the destination – Ubiquity!
Dissolving you, this dusk-and-dawn absolves you,
Leaves nothing more to be said.

AGING IX

1

In leaden light of another year
A whirlpool opens on ground that was home
To suck in the grasses that grew there,
Bulbs proved perennial, saplings for expectation;
Then the relics that furnished a house,
The made, inherited, looked for, kept for the record.
Down go the rows of books,
Headstones if not re-read, some weathered,
The piles, the files of papers –
Food for the vacuum, sheet by sheet.
It rips from the walls a lifetime's pictures,
Reduces to debris conjunctions held dear.
Digests them? For what renewal, for whose?

Still we stay, you and I, together.
But, memory stripped to a bare cell,
Waiting-room, anywhere, for a train delayed,
Can't trust the few sounds that reach us,
So deeply gurgling that natural shredder gulped.

2

Down goes the conscientious prose, the verse
Once needed, yet a curse
When blocked as when released
By one more angel-beast
In vain defiance of the daily news. –
Things with a silence in them the vortex may refuse.
Trust those, my mortal muse,

One co-progenitor
Of all that could move behind a single door,
Dark continuity
Far less of us, them, me
Than the bare verb to be.
Locking it, love, for my sake minimize
Even the genuine sighs.

URGENT REPAIR

That morning the car would not start
As a residual favour the garage man
Was induced to come to the house.

'I'm sorry,' he said when he'd looked,
'It's case for the carburettorologist,
Perhaps with a complication
That would have to be referred
To the senior electronitrician,
Specialist in the inner circuit
Separate from the outer that serves the lights –
Which you see are functioning.
Myself, I'm a tyriatrician
With some competence in exhaust pipes and bumpers;
And the consultants you need
Are at the central depot
Where parking space is restricted –
But so is the waiting-list, we are told,
To a maximum of one year ...'

'What?', I managed to interject,
'Only months ago you still knew
What makes the whole machine move – or stall.
You can't have forgotten that.'

'The whole?', he laughed. 'Where have you been?
Well, you're elderly, as the lingo has it.
And so is your vehicle, one of the also-rans.
Haven't you noticed? The whole is a hole in the system,
Pardon the pun, never again to be filled.
I've heard it whispered, however,
That somewhere someone is working on

A therapeutic supercoordinator –
Which couldn't be human either,
Could it, that ultimate robot-god,
Besides putting an end to another profession.
Meanwhile there may be those who still call themselves
GMs – your general mechanics –
Though you'll find that their expertise
Lies in having learnt what not to take on.

In due course your car could be towed...'

'Thank you. I'll think about it.'

        *   *   *

The longer I thought about it
The less urgent seemed the repair.
Oh, and the push-bike on which
With a girl friend on hers
I raced through blacked-out streets of bombed London,
Chased by a copper on his heavier mount,
Parting to fox him, give him the slip,
Is Pegasus now, transfigured:
Into freedom we felt we were riding then,
For freedom soon after joined up.

Immobilized now, one leg not fit
Either for riding or walking,
Our village shop and post office
Also things of the past,
The weekly bus about to be made redundant,
I rely on that mythic horse
Whether it flies or limps
And on love to transport me.

AGING X

(Dream Torso)

As psychopomp, not paediatrician now
Suddenly he was there, my father
Last seen when aged sixteen
Some sixty-six years ago
I was called to take my leave of him,
Last heard when his breath came rattling
Through walls and one floor of the house
In London, before the street
Was a bombed site, abandoned.

Bare presence, featureless,
It was he who conferred
With hospital bureaucrats
Emerging from their office,
To urge me kindly: 'Go
Down this long corridor
At the end of which you'll be met
By your doctors, a man and a woman.'

Weary, I walked it
Until the passage was blocked
By a locked door painted white,
Waited a decent while,
Then, wearier, made my way back
To where he stood and confirmed:
'Yes, a muddle, a misunderstanding...
Can you drive a taxi-cab?
We need to get to D.,
Where those doctors are based.'

A taxi? He'd kept no car, true.
Did he mean a rented one?

'I can't,' I had to answer,
Unable to explain
That more than a decade had passed
Since I gave up driving, let the licence lapse –
Or that this town he had named
Lay in an alien country,
Land of our fathers, Deathland.

Refusal truncated the plot,
Faint morning halflight withheld
The end like the beginning,
Left a locked door, painted white.

A CROSS-ROADS REVISITED

At the road-junction of a criss-crossed age
He stands, lone signpost to our heritage,
Signpost all cracked and jumbled like his book,
Both accurate, if patiently you look.
If not, a joker, you reverse his name,
LACSAP, he'll have the last laugh all the same.

Sixty-five years ago I studied it,
Then was diverted by the infinite
Too-manyness of living as of learning.
Marked on those pages now brittle, foxed, returning
Find passages that ever since marked me,
Though left unread, mislaid in memory;

So must indulge it here, his 'odious me',
Vessel of vanity, inanity
Yet the best premiss, apparatus, medium
For his own deep analysis of tedium
When mathematician, calculator still,
He'd reached the limit of his positive skill –

And in an ecstasy shifted from
Proud intellect's play with number, sign, abstraction
To plumbing of our greatest need, distraction,
Stripped bare the 'honnête homme'
More searchingly, relentlessly than Freud,
To prime for grace that ego–tripping void.

Apologist? Yes. But open to every doubt.
Crypto-indoctrinator? Yes. Without
Self-righteous quibbles, reasoning about
That beyond reason which we cannot know,

Power-driven certainty, the deadliest clout –
His arrogant 'angel become beast', but worse,
His and our global curse.
His faith? A gambler's throw
For ever against the odds:
But, nothingness your stake, the game is God's.

Stripped bare his language too, preferred
The plainest, driest word.
The sap he lacked, renounced, was eloquence
In love with its pretence;
Mistrusted poets, damned imagination
He did not lack – nor vision
His clipped words could let through, placed with precision.

'Diseur de bons mots, mauvais caractère':
At this bon mot – it could be Baudelaire –
I have to smile in wry commiseration,
Move to his blanks, the silences, meet him there,
The space he cleared, illumined by negation.

IN DETENTION

Somewhere, beyond these walls,
All range, all comprehension ever,
A light shines, justice.

Counted, do days grow weightier?
They dwindle, hollowed out because
We are not in them, severed from the flux
Of past to future, its moods and modes
Called present, waterfall, weir or dew-pond merely,
Spring, inlet, whirlpool, sea tide and current.

The law's arithmetic,
Its minus-plus accounting
Leave blunt the scythe-blade
Whose whetstone honed real time.

From our domestication
We may have strayed, marauding.
But caged here, languish,
Only when dreaming crave the counterblast,
Release of what remains of those
Who've learnt their lesson
And when not numbed are fiercer or more cunning;

Learnt there's no start, no finish
To such diminishment,
False continuities imposed
By the haphazards of conviction,
Power's ledgers of right and wrong –
However altered, cancelled, over-ruled,
Differences equipoised, the balance nil.

Somewhere a light shines, not for them nor us.

ECHOES

August autumnal, eyesight watery, blurred
With cataract, glaucoma,
Hearing three quarters gone,
Some good thread holding, webless I've hung on,
Still can breathe in this myrtle's deep aroma
Patchouli-dank, once aphrodisiac
From pale galactic lights against near-black –
By that out-staying stirred.

Elsewhere all's blast inflicted,
Blind retribution's blundering machines,
Tit for tat random, turned promiscuous:
Death dance of 'them' and 'us'
Till the floor crumbles, both in smithereens,
Long-suffering Earth the poorer for the skill
Spent on refinements of such overkill
Or damage done for gain as unrestricted.

Forgiveness, faith, hope, love?
Power's dupes defer them to far heavens above
While from our atmosphere
Winged heralds disappear,
Before few gathered for departure here
Not one swift, swallow, martin seen or heard
By those with minds receptive, senses clear,
Still learners of the what within the word.

'Look where you're going!' – 'Listen when you're addressed!' –
These are no loss to me,
But features known too well for eyes to see,
The too familiar tree
Most present to me when its bark was burning,

Whole seasons, years marked mainly by their turning,
Left blank, called silence, small throbs of the air and sea –
As though by seeming rest in constancy
Like news reporters I'd been unimpressed.

To other poverty I can be host,
Shut, shelve the books that log past expedition,
Clutter of shed ambition,
Aware how little baggage is enough –
Less where the tracks are rough –
And so much closer to the books' condition,
In only touching the residual stuff
May hobnob with a ghost.

Wondering at jumbled echoes of things occurred
Or not occurred, to come or not to come –
Whose cry? Whose bragging? Thunder? Kettledrum?
Crash of leaved branch? Mere thrum of life in coma? –
Now I'd be also dumb,
Into coherence never could blend those
Did not re-echoing verses recompose,
Though in arrears, an aggregate grown absurd.

THREE MOMENTS, SKETCHED

I

End of October, frost
Holding off in daylight,
Red admirals gather, dip,
Fluttering mark what season
To feast on rotting pears
Chucked on the compost heap –
They that rarely had sucked
The buddleia's nectar, disdained?

Sated, how can they winter
And where, invisibly?
Does the late sunshine lie?
Is it to death they're drinking?
They quiver off questions more vain
Than all that could befall them
Who will never have known the name
Of the wings we call them by.

II

Elongated, the torso, legs
With greater strides than ever
They made for home;
But the head shrunk
To a doorknob added
Less for use than propriety,
As a child might affix it,

Slowly down the lane
To late welcomings, partings
How lightly, silently
This giant shifts worn limbs,
Then halts, lying flat
And brainless on the tarmac!
So a child would have wondered
At his morning shadow, shorter.

III

November now, half moon
Clear in cleansed air, colder,
So desultory then the sunshine
That even by noon to us
It seemed as unemployed
As the showers in between
On to leaves falling fast
From boughs not yet bare.

If an order ruled it was
The wind's, only the wind's
That rips a green leaf free,
Shivers a slanted beam
Through the leaved boughs bending,
Shakes raindrops down from these
To make food of the fallen,
Feed the still standing tree.

SLEEP'S VESSEL

So changeable now, it may be the TITANIC
Abuzz with hubbub of the guzzlers, dancers,
Music laid on for those,
Vanity's microcosm
Powered by an engine hidden, muted, money;
Lone sculling-boat else, canoe, then submarine
Kelp for lithe pleasure-ground,
The bearings, mission dream –
Pre-lethal too, not Lawrence's ferry yet.

By day, by night, 'Embark!' is the one call
No matter to what landfall, destination
In any dock, on any beach or bed,
For all are in it, the loved, the sought, the dreaded
Throughout a lifetime and beyond its purlieus
Which a cold flux erodes:
Though never a captain, coxswain, purser speaks
The shallowest boards hold everything ever needed.

Oppression, pain break in, the craft reverts
To what its mortal fittings can and can't,
Becomes a space that's walled
Against rain torrent, billow, current, whirlpool, ice.

Merge in them, move! comes the imperative,
Straight, listing, on or down,
Steered or adrift, nobody's, water's way.

Poetry by Michael Hamburger from Anvil

Collected Poems 1941–1994

Reflects more than half a century's dedication to poetry and
constant engagement with both the natural and human world.

Late

A narrative sequence, both an elegy for and a celebration of
life towards the end of the millennium.

Intersections

Poems written between 1994 and 1999, meditating on the
intersections of past and present, continuity and change.

From a Diary of Non-Events

A year in the poet's life, blending observation of changes in
the natural world with daily life in and around his Suffolk
home, as the larger concerns of the outside world intrude.

Wild and Wounded

Poems written during 2000–2003, in which both political and
personal concerns deepen the timbre of his meditations.

*'Few English poets of our day can have come to their craft with the
cultural and linguistic richness of Michael Hamburger ... a thor-
oughly European, even cosmopolitan sensibility who is at the same
time a nature poet of thoroughly English stamp. A Brechtian social
and political satirist co-exists, and not always peaceably, alongside
a knowledgeable naturalist who dwells among the cloudscapes and
birdsong of Suffolk ... As a translator, of course, but also as a
distinctive, wide-ranging poet, Hamburger has been more than
usually attentive to the divisions, to the "shocks and conflicts" of
his century; his work helps us share in them, and enriches our
understanding.'*

STEPHEN ROMER, *Agenda*